Dorothy Menge

Things Happen When Women Care

Read December - 1986

by Marie Frost

STANDARD PUBLISHING
Cincinnati, Ohio   3217

SUMMIT CHRISTIAN COLLEGE

Cover Photo

© U.C.C. by Robert C. Hayes
All Rights Reserved

Library of Congress Cataloging in Publication Data

Frost, Marie.
    Things Happen When Women Care

    1. Witness Bearing (Christianity)—Case studies.
2. Frost, Marie.   I.   Title.
BV4520. F76   248'.5'0924   79-63323
ISBN 0-87239-346-1

© 1979, The STANDARD PUBLISHING CO., Cincinnati, Ohio.
Division of STANDEX INTERNATIONAL CORP.
Printed in U.S.A.

Acknowledgment is made
to Mary McCann for her able
assistance in preparing this book.

Preface

Once upon a time I envisioned for myself a noble ministry. I would become a missionary on the foreign field. Ever since I was a child I had heard of the desperate needs in China, India, and Africa. I couldn't imagine any way of doing more good than bringing the Word to these poor unenlightened people.

One preacher-husband and five children later, it appeared that my duties were to center around the church ladies' society. Instead of spreading the Word in an exotic language, I was destined to dole it out two syllables at a time to a steady stream of 3- and 4-year-olds in Sunday school.

It didn't take me long to discover that God really did want to use me as a missionary, though certainly not in the way I had dreamed. The first indication of this "call" came to me when I was a new bride. I was knocking on doors in a traditional church visitation program. I was expecting merely to hand out church bulletins telling people about our Sunday services. But I am naturally friendly and inquisitive, and these "formal" calls usually became neighborly chats. It was actually fun getting to know so many new people, inviting them to our little church, and enrolling their children in our Sunday school.

I was hardly prepared for the barrage of human needs that my simple friendly inquiries uncovered. More often than not I found people who were struggling with hurts, hostilities, depression, family problems, even serious illness or financial disaster, ready to open up to anyone who cared and was willing to listen. Often someone who had not attended church for years would come simply because I extended a personal invitation. Almost without my realizing it, I had accepted God's invitation to be a missionary—though my service consisted in sharing a sympathetic cup of coffee with a neighbor rather than fighting infections in a rice paddy. My role was to be a listener, to care, and to suggest God's way as the solution to the person's problem.

Whether you label this "outreach," "getting involved," or simply doing the job God gave you as a part of your human existence, you can't begin to be concerned about others without discovering that the need is endless. This book gives only a few representative experiences from my own life. Every day brings new encounters with people who want a friend, a confidante, perhaps a counselor. I begin by being a friend, and let God direct matters from there.

All the "case histories" in this book are true stories, except for changed names. Because of this, the questions following each story can be used for discussion. There are no "textbook answers." Several basic principles do emerge, however, and I offer them here in the hope that they may guide you as you reach out to share God's love with others:

1. Don't just "stick to your own kind." Widen your circle of contacts to include those who need help.

2. Go out of your way to be a friend. Be generous with your time and invitations.

3. Find a common interest. Anything from needlepoint to auto mechanics could serve as a springboard to a more meaningful friendship.

4. Be alert for opportunities to channel conversations along spiritual lines. Sometimes this happens in a first encounter;

more often it takes time—weeks, months, or even longer.

5. Don't condemn someone else's lifestyle or theology. Be positive. Find something with which you can agree. Then whenever practical introduce the Christian way of life as presented in God's Word.

6. Start "where they are." Don't give a person more information than he is prepared to handle. Don't push.

7. Don't be discouraged. God's timing is different from ours.

8. Pray more than preach. Ultimately, God is going to have to touch the person's heart. You can't accomplish it alone.

Marie Frost

Contents

		Page
1	Dick — Far-Out!	11
2	The Browns — Childlike Faith	15
3	Mrs. Rose — My Failure	21
4	The Collingsworths — The Warily Interested	27
5	Meg — The Insecure Neighbor	37
6	Phyllis and Roger — Domestic Discord	43
7	Brenda — God's Sense of Humor	49
8	Joan — The Self-Sufficient	53
9	Janet — The Overachiever	59
10	Jim — The Hostile Husband	65
11	Susan — The Three Hours on a Train	73
12	Mrs. Jason — The Dying	77
13	The Gardiners — In Despair	85
14	Cappy — "Let There Be Light"	91
15	The Merricks — Freedom Through Forgiveness	99
16	Vacation in "Paradise"	105
17	Mr. Juarez — Above Tragedy	113
18	Louise — A Job Done Well	119
19	The Bradleys — The "Surprise" Party	125
20	Stephanie — One Link in the Chain	131
21	Heather — Lost, One Coat; Found, One Friend	137

Chapter **1**

Dick — Far-Out!

Tina VanDermaa was dramatically outspoken. I used to wince at her colorful language and her pagan social involvement (she was a former stripper). But she attended our church, and at one of our evening services she committed her life to Christ. Forthwith she became a flaming evangelist!

Most people were impressed with Tina's total turning from her former ways. But not so her husband Dick. He wanted nothing, but nothing, to do with Tina's newfound religion.

On one occasion when I stopped to see

Tina, I decided to get acquainted with Dick. I found him under their car, trying to fix a broken tail pipe. I peeked under the car. "Hi, Dick." I said.

"Hi, yourself," he said. "What in #$¢*% are you doing here?"

"Trying to help you fix the car," I ventured.

Though Dick had no idea who I was, he said, "Well, hand me that ¢*#$@ wrench over there as long as you haven't anything better to do."

Between Dick's profanity and the unmuffled motor, we didn't do much communicating, but he really didn't seem to mind my watching him. Eventually he got out from under the car and I introduced myself.

Dick wasn't sure what to think after he found out that this nosey lady was the preacher's wife, but I assured him I appreciated the chance to meet a fellow Dutchman. At least we had that in common!

I went out of my way to become Dick's friend, chatting with him whenever I came to visit Tina. We never discussed religion, or church related activities, but I did notice that he curbed his speech when

I was there.

One Sunday many months later, wonder of wonders, Dick attended an evening service. We chatted, as usual, and I concealed my absolute amazement that he had decided to come.

From that time on, Dick attended services regularly; and finally he professed a personal faith in Jesus Christ. After making this commitment, Dick came to me and made this remark: "One of the things that kept me coming was your interest in me as a person—not just as a soul!"

Dick's drive and rough-and-tumble manner made him a natural athlete. When he volunteered to take over our boys' club, our gym could hardly accommodate the number of enthusiastic members. Dick faithfully worked with those boys for several years. When he was transferred to another city, it was our loss but another church's gain. Dick continued his youth work in his new church home.

As I think back to my meeting with Dick, I'm so glad God didn't let his cantankerous spirit turn me off. I'm beginning to realize that an agitated soul is often closer to the kingdom than a passive one.

Points to Consider
1. What do you think of the way I introduced myself to Dick?
2. Do you have any friends you love for their own sake, whether or not they share your religious beliefs?

Chapter 2

The Browns — Childlike Faith

Over the years, I had accumulated a lot of white elephants. Looking over the assortment, I decided some of them had to go. I placed a "miscellaneous for sale" ad, listing among other items a metal bed.

Mrs. Brown, wife of a local attorney, arrived to inquire about the bed. An elderly relative had come to visit and had been taken suddenly ill. She needed the bed immediately.

As she looked at it, I looked at it, too. It really didn't look saleable—somewhat saggy and definitely rusty. "I can't even charge my $2.00 asking price for that," I said, "but if it will help you, you are welcome to take it."

Mrs. Brown seemed to find this gesture overwhelmingly generous. Evidently she was not used to people giving things away. At any rate, because of the emergency and my insistence, she gratefully took the bed and went on her way.

Some time later, Mrs. Brown called us. The relative had died, and, since they had no church affiliation, she wondered if my husband would conduct the funeral. This he agreed to do.

I recall that the service at the funeral home was rather unusual. The whole group seemed to be unfamiliar with any sort of church procedure, and my husband had quite a time silencing the chatter of the "audience" so he could pray about the deceased. But his words must have carried some weight, for after the funeral Mrs. Brown asked if I would come and visit her the following day. "I want to talk to you," was all she said.

I stopped in on my way home from a Sunday-school teachers' meeting where I had been demonstrating classroom aids.

"I asked you to come here," she said, "because your husband's message opened up a whole new world for me. I have never been religious—in fact we've never gone to church at all—but it surely seems I need to know something more about the Christian way of life."

In the car I had a flannelgraph and figures that I had used at the teachers' meeting. It suddenly seemed practical to show Mrs. Brown the "Christian way of life," as she called it, via this simple flannelgraph, childish though it might appear to this rather sophisticated woman. Using her couch as a backdrop I arranged the pieces, explaining why Christ came to die for us and how we can be assured of forgiveness through His sacrificial death.

Not only children respond to visualized messages. Mrs. Brown was exuberant in her response. "You make it so plain," she said. "What a beautiful story of God's love, and it even includes me! Thank you for telling me." And on the spot, in simple childlike prayer, Mrs. Brown asked Jesus to be her Savior. Perhaps this is not so surprising as it seemed at the time. Mrs. Brown *was* at the very beginning level, religiously speaking!

Before I left, I asked if she would like my husband to come and share God's message with her husband. "Oh, that isn't necessary," she beamed. "If you leave those pictures of the cross, Jesus, and Heaven, I'm sure I can tell him how to get there. And I'm sure he will want to know." Of course, I gladly left the figures with her.

The next Sunday found both Mr. and Mrs. Brown at our service. Their radiant faces told me that they *had* learned about the "Christian way of life." They progressed rapidly from this beginning, studying and growing and becoming staunch in their adult faith. And why had these extremely receptive people waited so long to accept Christ? Because, quite literally, no one had ever told them about Him.

On my own, I would not have set out to make converts armed with a rusty bed and a flannelgraph, but obviously God had selected those "tools" and used them for His purpose. I was glad He used me, too.

Points to Consider
1. Is there more at stake at times than a "shrewd business deal"? Discuss.
2. How many different ways did God use to interest the Browns?

Chapter 3

Mrs. Rose — My Failure

I debated whether to include this story, because none of us likes to face up to failure. But nothing could more graphically illustrate what can happen when "no one cared," even temporarily. Mrs. Rose's tragedy has at least had the effect of making me superconscious of the importance of caring, even in little things.

Mrs. Rose was a member of our church. We were friends, having become acquainted through our monthly women's meetings. She was a fragile and sensitive person, a lover of art and poetry, who sometimes seemed almost remote from our workaday, catch-as-catch-can world. I often visited her; it was a treat to sit in her perfectly manicured garden sipping afternoon tea from china cups. She was the perfect hostess.

On one of my first visits, Mrs. Rose had expressed a deep need to know Christ more than "just as a friend." I felt that I helped her meet that need by talking to her about God's loving concern for her through His Son Jesus. After that, she began attending a Bible study group that I conducted on Sunday mornings.

The Roses had a daughter, little Cindy, an obstreperous four-year-old. Cindy seemed to be more than Mrs. Rose could handle. The child had early learned to overcome her mother's gentle remonstrances with strong-willed resistance; the result was the too familiar one of a child controlling a parent.

One Sunday morning Mrs. Rose came into our Bible study class dragging a screaming and kicking Cindy behind her. She was obviously making an attempt to be firm and ignore Cindy's tantrum, but Cindy was not about to give in. It was impossible for me to conduct any sort of discussion over this uproar; I was surprised that Mrs. Rose had come at all under the circumstances.

"Perhaps you could take Cindy down to the preschool class," I said, kindly as possible. "I'm sure she'll be happier there."

Wordlessly, Mrs. Rose got up and led Cindy from the room. As she passed me, I was struck by her look of total anguish, almost as if she were saying, "You, too, are turning on me."

I continued the class, but I felt bewildered by that look. I hadn't been rude; in fact I had been as tactful as possible. Why had my action had such a dramatic effect on the woman?

"I'll stop at her house this afternoon and talk with her," I promised myself. "Whatever was wrong, I'm sure I can make amends." But the day was a typically busy Sunday; there was no time for a visit.

After the evening service, which the Roses did not attend, I thought of her again. "I'll go first thing in the morning," I promised myself.

Just then the telephone in the church office rang. I could tell from my husband's voice that something bad had happened. "That was Mr. Rose," he said quietly. "His wife just committed suicide."

I sat there numb. What had happened? Did I have a part in it? At that moment, I was only conscious that I had meant to visit her, had put it off for a few hours, and those hours proved to be the crucial ones for her. My guilt was almost overwhelming. Momentarily I forgot that God does not hold us accountable for another's destiny. It is Satan who is our accuser and would wish us to dwell on our failures.

Later I learned the whole story of Mrs. Rose's day. When she arrived at my class, Cindy in tow, she had just come from the preschool class. Half an hour had been spent trying to force the child to attend. My innocent and reasonable suggestion was her "last straw." "Even Mrs. Frost didn't help me," she told her husband after her return home.

The afternoon proved even more frustrating than the morning for Mrs. Rose. She was trying to organize a birthday party for Cindy (ironically enough!) and everything went wrong. No one had time to drive her to the store to pick up the forgotten birthday candles, the table wasn't ready, the guests were due. In her hysterical frenzy, she went to the basement and hanged herself.

"Obviously unbalanced," you say. Of course. In the end, the most trivial things proved to be her undoing. But would an equally trivial event—a ten-minute visit from me—have proved to be her salvation? I can't know for sure, but I will always remember that I didn't make that visit.

Points to Consider
1. Do you think I was carried away with the significance of the class I was conducting, rather than the needs of an individual?
2. How could I have better handled this situation?
3. What does God's Word say about guilt?

Chapter 4

The Collingsworths — The Warily Interested

It all began when Donna's car skidded on the ice in front of her house. I was on my way to the grocery store and stopped to offer her a push.

"I guess I was in too much of a hurry," she said. "I was on my way to see Mother. She's in the hospital with a broken hip."

"I'm so sorry," I sympathized. "My husband is a minister, and he visits at the hospital. Would you like us to visit your mother when we're there?"

"How kind of you," Donna replied. "I think Mother would be delighted!"

But my good intentions didn't materialize, and Donna's mother was home before I made my visit. One day I decided to stop by to see her at her house, and there I found Donna, busily searching through a stack of religious books.

"Isn't it odd that you should stop by today," Donna remarked. "I've come to a point in my life where I'm really interested in finding a religion that means something. I've been a churchgoer because it seemed the thing to do—but last year I stopped going. Showing up for Sunday services didn't seem to have anything to do with God at all. Even the services didn't say much about Him; the church seemed to be more of a social organization. I have a feeling that there must be a better way, and I'm going through these books to see if I can find some sort of guidance." I noticed that several of the books were on cults. Donna certainly had picked up a varied collection of thought here!

Donna found it "odd" I should stop by at this particular time; I suspected "providential" might be a more accurate word. Perhaps God and I were to take this opportunity to get *His* case across to this searching woman.

It is a rare, awe-inspiring experience to come upon such a direct need for spiritual counsel. Usually I know someone for weeks or months on a superficial basis before religion ever enters the conversation. Here, religion was the immediate bridge of communication between two relative strangers.

Even though Donna was indicating this interest, I knew that it was not my job to begin quoting the Gospel of John and preaching salvation to her. Our rapport was fragile and tentative, and I didn't want to destroy it. So, casually, I picked up one of the books. "There are so many religious books printed today, it's no wonder people get confused," I offered. "I'd be interested right now to know what you think about God and Christ, rather than what these books say. What do you think it means to be a real Christian?"

Donna seemed pleased that I valued her opinion. Her answer was simple and direct: "I'm sure it means going to church, reading your Bible, and tithing." She laughed self-consciously at the last item. Donna was a wealthy woman, and more than used to being approached for worthy causes.

"These things are all true," I agreed, "but a real Christian is one who trusts Christ in a *personal* way."

Eagerly, Donna pressed me for more details. "How do you know this is true? How does it work out in real life?"

As we talked, I explained a bit about my own experiences, how I know that God really cares about each person, how we really can find His answers in the Bible. The more we talked, the more enthusiastic Donna became. "Do you think this is perhaps the answer you're looking for?" I ventured.

"I thought I was a Christian when I went to church," said Donna, "but it wasn't the way you describe at all. I want to be that kind of a Christian. Do you think I can?"

We had almost forgotten Donna's mother seated in the corner. But she hadn't missed a word of the conversation. "Can I be a Christian, too?" she piped.

"Everyone can be a Christian," I said. "The Bible teaches 'Whosoever will, may come.' All we have to do is ask Jesus to take over our lives, follow His directives, and let His will have power over ours."

The three of us prayed a simple prayer of faith together. Actually, there were four of us in that room. God had joined me on this friendly morning visit, and used it for His own purpose.

On this rather dramatic note, the Collingsworths' story began. Donna came to church regularly, and soon joined a Bible class. Gradually her entire life focus began to shift from its former social-oriented routine to more perceptive, gentle, person-centered relationships. Remembering her initial encounter with Christ, I was overjoyed to see Him working in her life just as she had asked Him.

I was not the only one watching Donna's progress. Her husband Thurston, a high-powered success in the financial world, found his homelife becoming unaccountably more tranquil. Donna was meeting the daily frustration of social commitments, in-law tensions, and a husband who was not always easy to live with in an altogether new manner. Where she might have shouted before, now she murmured. Conflicts were often resolved before he was fully aware they existed, because Donna could cope with them—in a kind but firm manner. She seemed to be getting more positive and confident. What was going on? Whatever it was, he was benefiting.

Donna tried to explain that Christ had come into her life and actually changed her value system. Thurston, anxious to show support, decided that if religion was what Donna wanted this season, he would help the cause. He promptly purchased two hundred Bibles and presented them to her—in case she wanted to give them to anyone, or do anything with them, or something . . . He then turned back to his business, prepared to forget about the whole thing.

Thurston had lived a full and successful life—or thought he had. But God obviously felt that now was the time for Thurston to begin to put his many talents to better use. Thurston—in spite of himself—became interested in Donna's "new" way of life. He became aware of the void in his own life that really was not filled by business or even family and friends. Was he, who prided himself on being in touch with everything that was going on, missing out on something really important? Donna knew better than to push—but she hoped, and prayed, and waited.

One day Thurston found himself in the hospital being treated for a minor but persistent infection, with nothing to do but lie there, rest, and think.

We dropped in to visit him, at Donna's request. He was full of questions. Not the simple one Donna had asked, "How can I become a Christian?" but rather "Why should I?" He was well-read and knowledgeable, and I listened while my husband met Thurston's metaphysical arguments with equally metaphysical logic. Suddenly I heard myself saying, "But why do you make it so complicated when it's really so simple? It boils down to this. You have a need. God has an answer, and Jesus Christ is that answer. Turn your life over to Christ. He's the only one who can give you this peace."

"But," Thurston protested, "I can't feel it. There's nothing I can grab hold of. I can't see it or understand it." Thurston was too used to controlling everything to submit gracefully to an unseen Power.

"That's where faith comes in," I persisted. "The Bible says, 'Faith is . . . the evidence of things not seen.' Faith is a gift that is free for the asking. All you have to do, Thurston, is accept. Just invite Christ into your life without trying to analyze. Just make up your mind to follow Him."

Thurston was mulling this over as we left. He still appeared to be far from convinced. Yet, I really wasn't too surprised when we received an excited phone call from him the next day. "I understand now!" he exulted. "I've been reading my Bible, and I understand what it means to be a Christian!"

"God certainly caught a lively fish this time," I couldn't help thinking to myself.

Time has proved this to be true. Thurston, like Peter, is an enthusiastic Christian whose zeal occasionally outstrips his prudence. His former cronies have been treated to a number of evangelical messages; Thurston has no patience with the subtle approach. "I don't know why I can't pound it into their heads!" he will rant. But while his speeches don't appear to be getting anywhere, Thurston's altered way of life is making an impression on his associates. And, like Peter, I suspect that Thurston will probably succeed in great measure in spite of his methods. He's been a super salesman all his life.

Points to Consider

1. What would have happened if I hadn't stopped to help Mrs. Collingsworth? Since I missed visiting her mother in the hospital, I could have just forgotten about it. What would have happened then?
2. What clues were there that Mrs. Collingsworth was ready to accept Christ as her Savior?
3. Mr. and Mrs. Collingsworth's stories were very different. How did we meet their respective needs? What can you see in this story that indicates God working through us?

Chapter 5

Meg — the Insecure Neighbor

Meg and her family moved next door in late July. I dropped by to introduce myself and welcome her to the neighborhood. She was embarrassed to meet "the preacher's wife," since she had been drinking. But she offered me a cup of coffee and we had a nice chat. The family was a "his and hers" setup, with five preschoolers between them. "These kids are driving me crazy," Meg wailed as little Tad climbed all over her. It didn't help the situation when he whiningly insisted on sharing Mom's beer.

"Perhaps you might be interested in enrolling some of the children in our Christian preschool," I suggested. Meg raised her eyebrows at the word "Christian," but she was desperate enough to consider the idea.

The following Monday morning Meg did indeed arrive at school, and enrolled Matt and Joanie. Both children adjusted quickly, and in a few weeks Tad joined the group. Since it was convenient for me to give them a ride, I saw Meg almost daily on a simple, friendly basis.

Except for her overabundance of preschoolers, Meg did not present the picture of the frowsy, harassed housewife on the brink of emotional disaster. She was attractive, poised, beautifully dressed, and competent. In fact, I was to realize as our relationship progressed that Meg was too self-controlled, too well-organized to realize why she found herself basically unhappy. I did begin to sense that Meg's fashionable facade was hiding a deep insecurity. Gradually she began to trust me enough to admit her feelings of inadequacy. "When I don't know what to do, I just give up and drink," she said one hot, steamy afternoon. "I'm not sure I should have remarried—now I'm responsible for five children instead of just my three. What if Bob walks out on all of us the way Jeff did?"

Meg's life was a history of hurts. Her mother had deserted her as a child, her first marriage failed, the second didn't look promising. She was fearful, almost expecting the worst to happen as a matter of course. Was there enough trust left in her to risk opening up to religion? I wasn't sure about Meg, but I didn't have any doubts about God! So . . .

"Several mothers from the preschool meet on Wednesday morning for Bible study," I said. "We discuss our personal problems and search for the answers God has provided in the Scriptures. Would you like to join us? I think you'll meet some other young women you'll enjoy knowing."

Meg seemed wary of my invitation, and I assumed that it was only her social consciousness that prevented her from refusing me outright. Much to my surprise (When will I learn?), she joined us the next Wednesday morning.

For the first several discussions, Meg was mainly an observer, a listener. But she continued to come, and one day she began to contribute. I could feel her reaching out, as if she were daring herself to trust this new force that was creeping into her life. Her husband was totally disinterested in the whole thing—would this create the fatal wedge in their marriage?

Fortunately, while Bob was not interested in religion, he was interested in Meg's welfare, though she didn't have enough self-confidence to realize it at this point. When she hesitantly mentioned a retreat for married couples that she would like to attend, he surprised her by agreeing to go along. After all, what could they lose by attending a few lectures and prayer sessions?

As it turned out, they lost a lot of selfish pride. Meg lost some of her hang-ups about her inadequacies. She also lost a lot of her fear of being deserted. When she phoned me the night they returned and said, "Now I understand what you've been talking about!" I knew God had gone along for the weekend. Meg had met Him head on, and He had turned her life around.

I've seen this happen too many times to be skeptical anymore. God does dramatically take charge of the lives of those who invite Him. But does this sudden burst of enthusiasm and faith last? Meg's turning point occurred over a year ago. Her husband has not become a Christian—yet, at least. But Meg has not only accepted Christ, she has accepted responsibility for herself. "When I stopped blaming other people for my unhappiness, and started trying to change my own life with God's help, I was no longer afraid or unhappy. Once I realized how much God values me as a person, I began to feel important. My children need me. Bob needs me. I have a job to do!"

And, of course, once Meg realized how much she could do and began doing it, she naturally began to reach out to others. She is an active church member, a Christian wife and mother. People count on Meg to help in times of need. The family is strong now and growing stronger—not without temptations and setbacks and frustrations, but, more to the point, never without God.

Points to Consider
1. What do you think would have happened if I had indicated any critical attitude toward Meg's drinking?
2. What common interest did Meg and I share?
3. How did God use me to help Meg begin to change her life?

Chapter **6**

Phyllis and Roger — Domestic Discord

Phyllis' teenage daughter Beth was my daughter's best friend, so naturally Phyllis and I became acquainted. She was a beautifully dressed, competent, take-charge type, very attractive. She was also very nervous—a chain smoker who found it impossible to sit and chat without fidgiting constantly.

As our acquaintance developed into

friendship, Phyllis revealed one of the causes of her nervousness. "My husband Roger needs help," she volunteered. "He has an extreme drinking problem. Can you, your husband, or the church do anything about it?"

I assured her that we would be happy to talk with Roger. She continued, "I love my husband very much, but I'm putting him on probation. This is absolutely the last time he can goof off. The next time he goes on a drinking spree, I'm leaving him. Don't you think it's about time I gave him an ultimatum?"

I wasn't sure my answer would please Phyllis, but I hoped it might be helpful in the long run. "You say you love Roger very much. The Bible has a lot to say about love, but nowhere does it suggest that we put loved ones on probation. We are to love others as God loves us—and God certainly doesn't put us on probation."

Phyllis looked at me as if I had struck her. "Well," she said vehemently, "so now *I've* been the one in the wrong all the time. *That's* an interesting twist! I thought giving him one more chance was generous!"

It was hard for Phyllis to imagine she had done anything that might provoke Roger into heavy drinking. But Phyllis was a domineering, strong-willed, self-sufficient woman. She was invariably right; Roger was always wrong. Roger, a highly intelligent, arrogant, irreligious man, was not about to have his life run by a bossy wife. This couple had created enough tension between them to drive him to drink and make her into a nervous wreck. And it appeared that neither of them had any idea of how their problems had come about. Phyllis obviously didn't, judging from her reaction to my statement.

After she regained her composure, Phyllis left. I was not sure I hadn't lost a friend. But like the surgeon who must cut to heal, I felt I had done the right thing in disagreeing with her "probation" plan.

Apparently Phyllis took to heart what I had said—or perhaps I should say, what God had given me courage to say. But it wasn't easy for her. I heard that she joined a Bible study group in another town and was seriously seeking help with her problems through God's Word. I could only pray that she would find it.

Six months later, Phyllis and I met again. I could sense a definite change in her. She seemed calmer, gentle rather than hostile, loving instead of judgmental. She had asked God's help in using her strong-willed determination as the tool to remake herself. God had certainly helped her, turning her drawback into a real asset.

Not long after that, Phyllis told me Roger had quit drinking—miraculously—almost overnight. Though she didn't say so, it appeared evident that once she had stopped dominating and nagging, his need to escape was gone.

Both Phyllis and Roger began attending church. They became close personal friends of ours and leaders in the church community. They have affected the lives of many others by giving help where needed, but more importantly by their own example of change.

"How grateful I am," Phyllis often comments, "that I never put Roger on probation!"

"And that God never puts *us* on probation," I reply.

Points to Consider

1. We often blame others for our problems. How was this true in Phyllis' case, or was it? Discuss.
2. Read 1 Corinthians 13 on love. Discuss God's standards of love vs. ours.

Chapter **7**

Brenda — God's Sense of Humor

God surely has to have a sense of humor as He watches us busily going around doing His work—our way! But let's face it, some days we don't feel very spiritual—only selfish.

This was one of those days for me. I climbed into my car, determined to take care of *my* interests and *my* errands only. "Today is my day," I said to myself. "No involvement with other people." Then, just to be sure God didn't interfere, I said half aloud, "To make me help someone today, God, you will have to put the person in the very path of my car—right in the middle of the road!" I was sure I was immune from divine interference after making that statement; but to be double sure, I decided to take a side street. Less traffic, I reasoned.

I hadn't gone three blocks when *right in the middle of the street* was a young mother pulling a coaster wagon in which were her two small children.

"But, God, this is *my* day!" I protested. Of course, I had agreed to stop if anyone was in the path of my car, hadn't I? And so, with a sigh, I stopped. And, as long as I had stopped, I got out of the car and introduced myself. "I've recently moved here," I said. "You must be one of my new neighbors."

"I'm Brenda Thomas," said the woman. We chatted for a few minutes about the neighborhood, her children, and what a lovely day it was. Then, realizing that God must have had in mind some purpose beyond calling my bluff, I mentioned, "Our church is starting vacation Bible school next week. Perhaps you might like to send your children, if they're not already enrolled somewhere else."

"Sounds super," was Brenda's reply. "I used to attend Bible school when I was a child. But since moving here three years ago, we haven't done much about attending church. We've been meaning to get around to it, but we hardly know where to begin."

"Why not visit us some Sunday morning?" I invited. She assured me they would.

And visit they did—the very next Sunday. They were impressed with the sermon and friendly atmosphere. "It's like coming home after all these years of being away from something really vital," Brenda remarked. Her husband's comments were equally enthusiastic. "I just can't believe we have been here for three years with this church right around the corner."

"I think God sent you my way," said Brenda. Though I didn't tell her exactly how right she was, I certainly had to agree.

Points to Consider
1. What does God say about being a joyful Christian?
2. Can we ever "take a vacation" from God? Can you think of any experiences in your life that were similar to mine?

Chapter 8

Joan — The Self-Sufficient

I met Joan at a Junior Women's League banquet several years ago. We were seated next to each other, and as the evening progressed we exchanged the usual background information. Joan told me that her husband had deserted her and their two small children. Now she was asking herself questions about who should be running her life, wondering what it would be like to trust her uncertain future to a God she wasn't sure was there. Her broken marriage had made it almost impossible for her to trust anyone. "I'll tackle it on my own," was one of her characteristic sayings.

At the time I met Joan, a leader of a popular cult had also sensed her need. He had been arranging weekly meetings to "enlighten" her and coerce her into his way of thinking. But so far Joan had remained unconvinced. She was still seeking, and she seemed to appreciate my friendly interest.

"Why not come over for lunch next Monday?" she asked. "I'd like to continue our discussion." I was free to come, and next Monday found me at Joan's house.

Mr. Fajema, the cultic leader, was there also. He'd stopped by to leave some literature. Needless to say, the three of us had an interesting time. When I suggested to Mr. Fajema that something he said was out of context—he had used a Bible phrase in a perverted way—he became sharp-tongued and ugly. How dare I challenge him! Evidently, his life was full of confusion and conflict in spite of his outward facade of loving equanimity. Remembering that I was a guest in the home of a recent acquaintance and not a participant in a theological debate, I withdrew from the controversy.

Time went on, and Joan and I continued our friendship. She had a sensitive, artistic nature, and I frequently stopped by to watch the progress of a painting she was working on in her spare time. I noticed a quality of haunting loneliness about the picture—almost as if Joan herself were crying out. Through her art she seemed to be saying, "I feel so alone. Aren't there any sure answers? Isn't there any secure place for me in this world?"

From time to time I left books with her that had helped me when I was searching for answers. Sometimes we discussed the books and I would try to answer her questions in the light of Biblical truth. I never saw her cultic friend again.

Joan had great empathy for the underprivileged, especially children. Because of her interest she invited me to attend a meeting where the speaker was a missionary to Korea, dedicating her life to work in an orphanage there. The orphanage had been bombed, and she had risked her life repeatedly to save the children. As she told her dramatic story, it was evident to us all that God's presence was more real to her than any natural fear could ever be.

That night God used His missionary as the instrument in bringing Joan's life to a spiritual climax. As I sat next to Joan, I heard her softly cry, "I need you, God. I'm tired of being alone. Forgive me for thinking I could control my life on my own."

And God, who is so ready to forgive, filled her life with hope and took away her loneliness. Truly, I did not leave that meeting with the same person who had accompanied me there.

I was hardly prepared for the drastic change that took place in Joan's life when she became a Christian. She had always been concerned for the physical needs of others, but now she searched for ways to make Christ real to those whose needs were spiritual. She might still take a cake to a neighbor, but now she would stay to talk, to care, to be a real friend.

Joan had hardly started on her new spiritual pilgrimage when she noticed a lot of back pain. After days of testing, the physicians agreed that Joan was a victim of bone cancer. They gave her little hope of life beyond six months.

What at one time would have meant

blind hopelessness for Joan turned into a springboard for her spiritual development. "The time is short," she said. "I've got to make up for lost time."

Almost immediately, Joan enrolled in an organization called "One Day at a Time." She became a volunteer, daily going to hospitals, giving words of encouragement to others who were terminally ill. Though Joan was given only six months to live by her doctors, God has extended that time to six years, a miracle in itself.

It is evident today that Joan has become more fragile, her pain more severe. Yet one never hears her complain. When the sick ask her, "Why are you so cheerful when you know you are so ill? You must be an extraordinary person." She quietly answers, "I'm just an ordinary person, but I have an extraordinary God."

Points to Consider
1. What were the major lacks in Joan's life? How was she trying to find meaning?
2. After we met, Joan found God. God strengthened her and tested her. Discuss.

Chapter **9**

Janet — The Overachiever

Janet was one of those women who could do anything. She was a gourmet cook, superb seamstress, a genius at arts and crafts. She was always engineering community affairs—efficiently. She was a farmer's wife, and the mother of four small children.

She was an active churchgoer and taught a Sunday-school class. Janet never missed a scheduled service. She was what most of us would consider a model Christian woman a pattern for all.

And, yet, Janet was frustrated. She really had not learned to distinguish between Christianity and churchianity. In her search for peace of heart, she drove herself to furious activity. It bothered me to see this talented person dissipating her energy in such a futile fashion. Although I didn't know her personally—only as the mother of one of the girls in my son's second-grade class—I wished I could do something to bring real peace into her life.

I saw an opportunity when Janet gave a demonstration on flower arrangement at one of our PTA meetings. Our church Mothers' Club was always looking for good speakers, so I decided I would invite Janet to share her skills with us. Since our meetings also included a time devoted to an inspirational message and spiritual discussion, I felt that perhaps Janet might take away some meaningful insights.

Before asking her to come as a speaker, I invited Janet to come to one of our meetings as my guest. She seemed interested, but on the day of the meeting she called to say that something had come up and she wouldn't be able to make it.

"I'm sorry," I said, "but I'll call you again next month."

The next month, Janet's schedule was still too full. And the next. And even the next. Still, as I saw her hurrying around town, children in tow, attending to this committee or chairing that bazaar, I felt that our group had something to offer her. So for seven months I repeated my invitation, and I received seven polite, friendly turndowns. In the process, however, Janet and I became friends, though our conversations were usually rushed as we moved in our separate busy circles.

By the eighth month, I had almost decided to give up on inviting Janet to our meetings. Perhaps I was jeopardizing our friendship by becoming a nag. This would be absolutely my last try.

Wonder of wonders, she came! And in a very beautiful way, God was there, too.

That evening, the lady in charge of the "inspirational message" selected a topic that seemed to speak directly to Janet. I don't even remember what it was; but as the group discussed it, offering their own insights and relating it to various Bible passages, Janet became totally engrossed. Such sharing was all new to her. By the end of the evening she was glowing with excitement.

"These women feel so free to talk about God in their lives. He's so real to them. I haven't thought about Him that way since I was a child."

Suddenly, Janet had a new view of her own church life. It was busy, but barren. How long had it been since she had really talked to God in a personal way? She gave Him service, but not attention. She was involved in church activities—over-involved, actually—but she had lost sight of the real reason for the church's existence. The church structure, not God, had become her top "religious" priority.

Our meeting had provided a new focus. God had used us to meet her need.

Janet's life began to change after that first experience. First of all, she didn't have to be invited to our meetings any more—she came, and learned, and shared. Gradually—one can't just leap out of a social circle in a single jump—she reorganized her life with God at the center.

Janet is still one of those women who can do anything. But now she selects her activities according to a different set of standards. She doesn't do "church work" any more; she does God's work.

"If I hadn't come to that Mothers' Club meeting, I might still be running around in circles," Janet often remarks. "Just think what might have happened if you had quit inviting me after my seventh refusal!"

Points to Consider

1. Discuss the differences between Christianity and churchianity.
2. Discuss persistence vs. pushiness vs. giving up too soon. What indicators were there that I could invite Janet repeatedly without offending her?

Chapter **10**

Jim — the Hostile Husband

Sarah Thatcher attended our church regularly, but no one ever saw her husband Jim.

"I wish you'd talk to Jim," Sarah said to my husband and me one Sunday morning. "He doesn't believe anything. He says he's an agnostic."

My first impulse was to visit the Thatchers so we could get acquainted with Jim. But it was a busy time, so it was actually several weeks later when we were able to stop by for a visit.

It was obvious from the moment we arrived that Jim had less than no interest in us. When we came through the front door, he disappeared through the back door. We made no issue of this disappearance, but had a pleasant visit with Sarah.

Some weeks later we had an excuse to try again. We had some Bible-school materials to leave for Sarah, who was one of our teachers. Once more Jim disappeared through the back door as soon as we arrived.

We hoped for an opportunity to meet Jim two weeks later when he attended the Bible-school program in the interest of his children. Though Jim came, he managed to avoid us all evening.

But Jim didn't quite manage to avoid God. The children's program was effective and moving, and Jim, who was an artist, found himself responding emotionally, though most unwillingly. He went home that night possibly more hostile than ever.

"All these Christians are alike," he said to Sarah. "They read the Bible and sing the hymns and say the right words, but when someone really needs help they're not about to put themselves out. They're just a bunch of phonies."

Sarah said nothing to this. After all, there was probably an element of truth in what Jim said. Who of us had not been guilty of turning away just when we should get involved? For the moment, the Thatchers dropped the subject of religion.

The very next week Jim had an opportunity to put his conclusions to a test. He heard that a waitress in his cafeteria was seriously ill. She had no one to care for her two small children, and it seemed that the only solution would be to put them up for adoption.

"Aha!" thought Jim. "I wonder what Sarah's preacher friend would do about this. Would he be willing to step out of his nice little pulpit and go into the street to do some real good?" In a surly voice he called us and challenged us to do something about the woman's plight—not stopping to think that God might be using him as an instrument for good! "What are you going to do about it?" he demanded of my husband.

"I'll be glad to help," was my husband's reply. "When and where can I meet you to talk about what we can do?"

"Downtown, my agency, any time tomorrow afternoon," was Jim's surprised answer.

They met and talked and planned. My husband was able to place the children in a church home for several months until the mother was able to care for them again. Nothing "religious" passed between the two men, but Jim did seem less blatantly antagonistic. *One* Christian had acted charitably *one* time, he had to admit.

Again weeks passed. Vibrations between the two Thatchers were not particularly harmonious. In a way, Jim seemed to be saying that the *one* incident was the exception that proved his point. It was not an easy time for either of them. But, as always, God was keeping an eye on the situation in His own way.

It was now winter, and Jim suddenly contracted pneumonia. He was very ill. After he passed his crisis he still had to rest in bed for three weeks. He did not want visitors. "Just leave me alone" was his not-too-encouraging command.

When Jim commanded, he usually got his way. Actually, he had a plan in mind for that enforced period of illness. Being an avid reader anyway, he decided to go through Sarah's Bible and outline his case against God and Christ—and finish this battle once and for all. For the next two weeks he read and read, writing copious notes to prepare for his planned confrontation with Sarah—and probably with us.

We knew nothing about this project, but as a matter of Christian concern kept the Thatchers in our prayers, both for Jim's physical recovery and for their peace of spirit as well.

And how did God deal with this antagonistic man? Perfectly, of course. He gave Jim time to read and think. And late one night Jim, who was intelligent in spite of his stubborn streak, realized that he was no longer arguing with the Bible, but agreeing with it. He had his confrontation, not with Sarah but with God himself—and it was a confrontation of love.

"I can hardly believe it!" he told Sarah. "It's the truth. God is real. I've been wrong!"

Truly God had moved in on Jim in His own time. All we had to do was pray, wait, and be willing to practice what we preached. He took care of the rest.

The very next Sunday Jim was at the morning service. His whole countenance had changed—surly, furtive Jim was no more. As if to make the transformation complete, *he* sought *me* out in the foyer after the service.

"My, you look so different," I commented. "You don't look as if you'd been ill at all."

"Thank God, I've never felt better in my whole life!" was his significant reply.

Points to Consider

1. What would your reaction be if you met someone like Jim?
2. No one could talk about God's love to Jim, but he could be shown God's love. How?
3. What do you think might have happened to the Thatchers if someone insisted on forcing a confrontation with Jim?

Chapter 11

Susan — Three Hours on a Train

Every day we come in contact with someone whose life touches ours only briefly. Yet, even these passing encounters can be significant.

On one occasion I boarded a train at Springfield, Illinois, en route to Joliet. I had hoped for three hours of peace and quiet, perhaps a chance to finish a book I was reading.

The train was full, but I was fortunate to find an empty seat next to a young lady who was also reading. "Good," I thought, "she won't want to talk and I'll be able to relax."

After a brief greeting, I settled back to read, but I couldn't concentrate. I glanced at what my companion was reading. The title, of all things, was "Questioning?" God seemed to say, "Aren't you going to ask her what she's questioning?"

I sighed and determinedly settled back in my seat. This time was *mine*. God should understand my need for rest. But obviously He didn't think it was as pressing as I did. No matter how hard I tried, I couldn't even get comfortable, much less concentrate on my own book.

Finally I ventured, "My, that looks interesting. Is it for a college course?" She looked like a student.

"You guessed right—I'm a college senior. My name is Susan Cox. But this isn't required reading. I have so many unanswered questions that I'm doing a little homework on my own."

Once again, I realized how simply God arranges opportunities for spreading His Word. I no longer felt weary; instead I was excited by this new contact.

"We all have questions," I said. "I'm

beginning to realize that only God has the answers for most of them."

"That's my dilemma," said Susan. "My biggest question is how can I know God?"

What a perfect opportunity to share with her the story of God's love! "God's interested in answering any questions we may have. He cares about all of us." For two hours we talked about Jesus Christ, why He came and gave His life for us.

By then I had reached my destination. Susan seemed to understand what God and I were trying to tell her. "Perhaps I can help if you have any more questions," I said, handing her a card with my name and address.

A few days later I was surprised to receive a letter from Susan. In part it read, "I am glad you witnessed to me . . . I had been thinking about things for a long time. I needed someone with faith to help me make my own leap of faith. Thank you so much."

All I could say was, "Thank you, God."

Points to Consider

1. Think about your own daily life. Might you be missing similar opportunities for meaningful "brief encounters"? Have you put too high a value on your own privacy?
2. How would you begin a conversation with a stranger with the idea that the talk might turn to religious subjects? (For a group discussion, you might set up hypothetical situations and practice various approaches.)

Chapter 12

Mrs. Jason — The Dying

One of our church groups had met on a Thursday morning for a "prayer and action" session. There had been a flood in our area, and after our prayer meeting we set out to help the victimized families.

As I was driving along on my errand of mercy, still remembering some of our prayers and filled with good intentions toward the flood refugees, I passed the Jason's house. I remembered that my friend Alice had told me that Mrs. Jason was very ill. I felt a sudden impulse to stop and see her. The practical, sensible half of me said, "Go on about your business," but the compulsion to visit this relative stranger was too strong.

I rang the doorbell. As I waited I thought back to a day three years ago when I had come here to visit the family, newcomers at that time. I had invited Mrs. Jason to our church, but she was definitely disinterested. Her main concern was the major home decorating project they had just begun. Now I was not prepared for the frail, shadowy Mrs. Jason who finally came to the door. "Please come in," she said. "I remember you. You are the lady who stopped here a long time ago."

I was pleasantly surprised that she remembered me at all. The house was lavishly and expensively decorated. "How beautiful it all looks now," I said sincerely.

"Yes, I've worked on it for three solid years, and now I can't take a thing with me," said Mrs. Jason. In answer to my perplexed look, she continued, "I just talked to my doctor, and he says I haven't much time left—perhaps only days."

Without stopping, she rushed on, "Can you tell me how to get ready to meet God?" She was plainly terrified.

I had never had this kind of experience before. Suddenly I panicked, as she looked furtively out of the window and said, "My husband is coming home in ten minutes. He wouldn't want to find a religious person here, so when he comes you'll have to leave."

What does one do in ten minutes to prepare someone else to meet God! I remember thinking that I was glad I had just come from a prayer meeting—I needed all the help I could get.

And, as always, when you need help and ask, God gives—in this case, sudden inspiration. Glancing at the beautiful crystal chandelier, I said, "Let's pretend that is Heaven—beautiful and totally right. Here we are (pointing to myself). But not one sin is allowed in Heaven, so that lets all of us out."

"Oh, but I don't play cards and I don't drink . . ." Mrs. Jason protested. She obviously had her own mental list of sins.

"The Bible doesn't enumerate those, but it does talk about pride and anger and other sins of disposition, and I know I've failed there," I said. "And, anyway, God's Word says 'All have sinned and come short of the glory of God.' "

Mrs. Jason listened attentively as I continued, "But God has some wonderful news for us." Taking my little Bible out of my purse, I placed it between us and the chandelier. "God provided a way for us to get into Heaven. Jesus Christ is that Way, because He's the only perfect person who ever lived." I pointed to the Bible as I spoke. "All we need to do is really believe this, and accept Christ's way to God. He says 'I am the way, the truth, and the life: no man cometh unto the Father, but by me.' "

Mrs. Jason needed no further convincing. Her time was short and her need was overwhelming. She simply asked, "How can I pray? I'm not able to kneel."

"God looks into the heart," I said. "Just ask Christ to forgive you, do the things He says, and let Him come into your life."

Since her husband was now coming up the sidewalk, I hurriedly left, promising her that I would return tomorrow. We would talk and I would answer her questions about becoming a Christian. She eagerly agreed to this.

I went home feeling rather inadequate. What could I say in the face of such a situation? Yet, I felt that just as I had been compelled to stop there, so perhaps I had been led to say something of value to Mrs. Jason.

Only hours later, we received a call from Mr. Jason. "My wife just passed away. She mentioned your visit, and I would like your husband to have her funeral."

As I hung up the phone, I felt devastated. Why hadn't I visited sooner? She lived only three blocks away. What had I forgotten to tell her? Had I helped at all in those brief ten minutes? In my momentary quandary, I lost sight of the fact that God takes our bumbling human efforts and makes something quite wonderful of them.

When I went to the funeral home, Mr. Jason was standing beside his wife's casket. When I introduced myself, his face became animated. "What did you tell my wife? She seemed to be at peace for the first time in her life. She wasn't even afraid to die. She was happy!"

"Oh, God, thank you," I prayed in my heart. He had taken my simple illustration and made Mrs. Jason able to understand.

Since Mr. Jason had asked, I repeated the same message I had given his wife, but sad to say he was not able to respond. In tears, he said, "I know you are right and my wife found her answer, but I'm not ready. If I accept this, I'll have to change my whole life. Later, perhaps."

Six months later Mr. Jason died of a heart attack. That, too, is in God's hands. Mr. Jason had heard the truth and at least intellectually recognized it. And God in His mercy may have used those words. Only He knows.

Points to Consider

1. Why do you think I stopped at Mrs. Jason's house rather than doing the good deed I had begun that morning? What if I had stifled my impulse to stop and gone determinedly on my preset course?
2. Which do you think was more important, my exact words or the fact that I was in the right place at the right time for God's purpose?
3. Did I fail with Mr. Jason?

Chapter **13**

The Gardiners — In Despair

There had been a tragedy in our town. A little boy had fallen from a moving car and been killed. I didn't know the family, but a friend of mine did. She asked if I would call on the mother. "She's so depressed, I can't reach her," my friend said. "Couldn't you try?"

I was certainly willing to visit Mrs. Gardiner and do whatever I could to help, though I wasn't sure what that would be. She was a very nervous young woman, and at this point she was understandably near hysteria. I tried repeatedly to tell her that God loved her and that her little boy was now in Heaven with Him.

"I know you want me to believe that," she said, "but I can't. All I can think of is my loss." I realized then that she was not interested in my words; she only wanted someone to listen and sympathize.

And so I listened! From the depths of her saddened heart, Sandy Gardiner poured out her story. "My husband was driving down the road," she sobbed. "The door wasn't locked and our little son opened it. He's gone, and Norm is so despondent because he feels it was his fault. He's an artist, but he's out of work now. All he does is pace the floor and brood. I don't know what we're going to do."

I listened compassionately, and she seemed somewhat calmed and comforted when I left.

I visited her often after that, and mainly I listened as she talked of her tragedy. Often, the mere talking about it takes away some of the trauma of such a shattering experience, and Sandy did seem to be stronger and more consoled each time I left. Basically all I could do at this point was be there, listen, and reiterate the fact that God loved her and had taken her child to be with Him in Heaven. In time, I felt, Sandy would accept the fact and resume her life.

One night I received a frantic phone call from Sandy. "Norm just called me from a hotel. He says he can't live with himself anymore and is going to commit suicide. I know he means it! Please, *please* help him!"

I hung up the phone, my head in a whirl. My husband was out of town. I had never met Norm. There were two hotels. Which one was he staying in? I had no idea.

At times like this the Holy Spirit gives us insights that are not our own. I picked up the phone and dialed the first hotel. I asked for Mr. Gardiner, praying that I would reach him and that God would give me the right words to say. And God did!

After my initial relief when he answered the phone, I blurted out the following: "Mr. Gardiner, my name is Marie Frost. I write children's books. I'm told you are an artist. Is there any chance you would illustrate a book I have just finished? I need someone desperately."

There was a long silence. "Please, God," I prayed, "don't let him hang up." Finally Norm spoke. "I think I'd like that. When do you need the drawings?"

Aware of the urgency for action, I said, "Just as soon as possible. I could even talk to you about them this evening if you are free."

Again, silence. "Please let him come," I silently pleaded.

"Yes, I think I can come this evening," came a hesitant voice. "Where do you live?"

I gave him directions, hung up the phone, and collapsed. "Thank You, God," I breathed.

Norm did come that night. We discussed the book and possible ways to illustrate it. I encouraged him when he made suggestions. It was easy to praise his work, for God had given him real ability. He left the house that night less morose, even with an air of tentative confidence. His final remark was, "You will never know how timely your call was."

Not long after that, Norm Gardiner became a Christian, led to his relationship with Christ by another artist who had had deep needs in his own life and had found

God to be his answer. Today Norm is a well-known artist for Christian publications, allowing God to direct his life. The tragedy that almost destroyed Norm proved to be the beginning of a fuller life for the Gardiners—all in God's time.

How aware I am that God is "not willing that any should perish, but that all should come to repentance." And how wonderful it is that God involves us in helping each other reach that all-important goal!

Points to Consider

1. What would have happened if I had not followed through on my friend's suggestion that I visit Mrs. Gardiner? What if I had dropped by only once and given up because she didn't want to listen to what *I* had to say?
2. Do you think it would have been more effective if I had called Norm and preached God's Word to him rather than offering him a job? Discuss.

Chapter **14**

Cappy — "Let There Be Light"

Our church had an active and popular women's club. It had grown over the years and had become a real vehicle for outreach. The format was a combination of devotional, educational, and "just for fun" activities. Many women who wouldn't have dreamed of joining a "church group" joined our circle for the social outlet it provided.

One such woman was young and successful Mrs. Baker. She wasn't at all interested in churchgoing, but she had come to one of our meetings as a guest of a neighbor. She became intrigued with, of all things, a lesson on cake decorating which was given by one of the members!

For me, Mrs. Baker's interest in cake decoration was a point of contact which might lead to a more meaningful encounter. If we were to enroll, for example, in a cake decorating class being sponsored by the local park district, we might become friends. Perhaps through such a friendship I would be able to lead her to the most important Friendship of all!

Although my own preference ran more to making a pan of brownies from a mix, I found myself approaching the Baker's home one afternoon, park brochure in hand, to invite Karen Baker to join the class with me.

The Bakers lived in a large country home, set back on a spacious lawn with several beautiful oak trees. The day was cloudy, but nothing could dim this scene. It was late October and everything was golden, bright, and beautiful—the perfect setting for the impressive house before me.

As I was about to ring the doorbell, a

pleasant-faced elderly lady came around the corner of the house. "What can I do for you?" was her friendly greeting.

"I came to see Mrs. Baker. She attended one of our club meetings, and I was hoping we could get better acquainted," I said.

"I'm sorry, Karen isn't home; she's at work. But I'm her mother, Dorothy Clarke. Won't you come in and visit with Cappy and me?"

I accepted her invitation, and soon I was gazing around a charmingly decorated country kitchen. Again I was struck by the beauty that surrounded this family. I began to realize that cake decoration would be just one more outlet for Mrs. Baker's obvious artistic ability. Everything looked absolutely picture perfect. "How nice for her family," I thought—a bit enviously.

Mrs. Clarke drew my attention to a man seated quietly beside the large window. "Cappy, we have a visitor," she said. "This is my husband, Cappy."

"How very kind of you to come and visit us," was Cappy's greeting. "Dorothy and I have been lonely since we moved here, and we're so glad for company."

"You may not have lived here long, but your home is certainly beautiful," I commented.

"Yes," said Cappy, "as I listen to the wind blow the falling leaves, I try to imagine the colors. I'm sure they're very bright right about now."

I realized that Cappy, surrounded by visual delights, was totally blind.

As I sat down beside him and we began to chat, Dorothy quietly disappeared—"to make a cup of tea." She seemed to sense that her husband needed someone all to himself for awhile.

Cappy was extremely depressed. "My world is so bleak," he complained. "I can remember when I could see, but it was so long ago. When I feel sun through the window, I try to remember light—if I could see even a bit of light it would be better than this awful darkness all the time!"

What could I say? I closed my eyes for a moment and tried to imagine never being able to see again. It was an overwhelming thought. I could only offer to this desperately unhappy man what I considered an equally overwhelming thought:

"I know someone who can give you

light," I said, "Jesus Christ. I am blessed with physical sight, but I have known a darkness in my soul—that horrible feeling of 'nothing there.' When I let Christ into my life, I got rid of that feeling of darkness inside me. I know that may seem minor to you with the cross you have to carry, but I also know what a tremendous difference it made to me." I continued, for Cappy was listening very intently: "Christ is called 'the light of the world.' The Bible says that 'in him is no darkness.' "

I said no more for a few moments, but once again God seized the opportunity to reach out into the darkness of one of His creatures. Cappy began to question me, and, as we talked about Christ and His loving vision, I felt that this man was daring to hope that perhaps he had found an answer.

Cappy did find his Light. That afternoon, before I left, we prayed together. In the weeks and months that followed, Cappy, his wife, and the Bakers all became Christians, receiving that special Light into their lives.

We never did take that cake decorating class. I suspect that God figured my efforts in that area might not be successful enough to establish a bond with the artistic Mrs. Baker. But He took my willingness and accomplished His purpose with it, creating an infinitely beautiful end result.

Points to Consider
1. Who was I concentrating on when I paid my visit?
2. Who needed help?
3. What do you think would have happened if I had not followed up on Mrs. Baker's visit to our club meeting?
4. What if Mrs. Baker's neighbor hadn't invited her to the meeting in the first place?

Chapter 15

The Merricks — Freedom Through Forgiveness

Arlene Merrick was the wife of a successful suburban physician. She and her husband had a busy social life, the usual wealthy, sophisticated crowd, and seemed to have little in common with us. This, of course, did not prevent my inviting her to a Bible-study group that met in her neighborhood. To my surprise she eagerly joined. She had long realized that her life-style was shallow, and through study with us she added the depth that can only come with an awareness of God's love.

Shortly after Arlene came into the church, she noticed a change in her husband's attitude toward her. It didn't seem to have anything to do with her newfound faith; but something was obviously bothering him that made him uncomfortable in her presence. He seemed depressed and withdrawn.

"Why don't you go and talk to my minister?" Arlene suggested to her husband. "If you can't talk to me, maybe you could talk to him and get some guidance."

Dr. Merrick somehow found the courage to do just that. One day he presented himself in my husband's office. He did have a problem, to be sure. He had been responsible for a young nurse's pregnancy and the abortion that followed. He felt guilt and fright in equal portions. "What if Arlene finds out what a mess I've made of my life?" was his way of putting it. "I love her, even though it doesn't look like it, and I don't want to lose her. Can you help me straighten out my life?"

"No, I can't help you," was my husband's answer. "Only Jesus Christ can do that. He can change your old nature, and He can give you new desires and the strength to withstand temptation."

"But can He forgive me? Can He give me another chance?"

"That's exactly why He came and why He died on the cross—to forgive us," my husband continued. As he talked about the comforting good news of salvation, Dr. Merrick in his need reached out to Christ, repented most sincerely, and vowed to start a new life obedient to Christ from that time forward.

In the initial exhilaration following his emotional decision, Dr. Merrick burst out, "I can hardly wait to share my faith with Arlene. Now I know what she's been experiencing!" And immediately he realized that he was about to face his first test. If he was going to share his joy with her, he was also going to have to share the sordid story that had precipitated the happy ending.

The two men prayed together and Dr. Merrick went off, strengthened but carrying his cross as well. He was determined to tell Arlene the whole story, from beginning to end, even though he would be running the risk of losing her.

When he had talked to his wife, her first statement was, "I can never trust you again!" She cried, she was bitter, she experienced all the shock of disillusionment, and, finally, she came to share her "disgrace" with me.

I could assure her of her husband's sincere desire to reform and to build a Christian future with her. I could try to help her by citing pertinent Scripture: How many times did Christ tell Peter to forgive his brother? Not seven, but seventy times seven! And what was the bald, simple fact of forgiveness? "If ye do not forgive, neither will your Father which is in heaven forgive your trespasses." Who can afford to be placed in *that* category?

She had come for comfort, and my words seemed harsh under the circumstances. But, of course, they weren't "my" words at all. As she left she possessed not only God's words but His ever-ready willingness to give the help that she needed for the problem at hand. I prayed that the Merricks would be able to accept God's help and solve their problem His way.

The very next day was our annual Sunday-school picnic. In sharp contrast to the activities of the past twenty-four hours, I was now involved in keeping the potato salad cold and finding cords for the three-legged race. I hardly expected to look up and see what I saw. There coming toward me were the Merricks arm in arm.

"Though it hurt, I'm so glad now that Ken was honest," began Arlene, just as he said, "Arlene has forgiven me and we're starting all over again!" He summed up the whole experience in a memorable statement: "Only Christ could make it possible. It's as if chains that I had worn on my ankles for ages have fallen off and left me free." And, of course, that's exactly what had happened—Christ had taken their chains of sin away and made them free in Him.

Points to Consider

1. If you have wronged someone, the need to make amends is obvious if not always simple to accomplish. But what about your responsibility to someone who has wronged you?
2. Can "sympathy" and "understanding" ever do more harm than good?

Chapter 16

Vacation in "Paradise"

Not long ago my husband and I spent two weeks at the Kobola Hilton in Hawaii. It was not our usual vacation—in fact it was a once-in-a-lifetime experience. This combination business and pleasure trip was our first visit to the islands, and we luxuriated in the perfect temperatures, lush foliage, and gentle trade winds. What a wonderful opportunity to get away from all the demands of the "real world" for awhile! Each morning we left our suite to sun ourselves on the oceanfront beaches or swim in the beautiful pool. If "rest and relaxation" were what we needed, we had certainly found the ideal spot for them.

Or had we? In this casual but wealth-oriented atmosphere, I found myself constantly talking to people; and I shortly realized that the people here in "paradise" had the same or worse problems than the people at home. I also could see that many of them were more than eager to talk—if only someone would listen.

From then on, I decided I was probably not meant to take a vacation from *every* aspect of my daily life. The fact that I was here at all was a culmination of a combination of events and circumstances. Perhaps God had had His usual hand in the arrangements! As a result, I talked with many searching people; helped a few direct their thinking toward Christ instead of cash; and realized that if I could do this all day for years I would still not begin to satisfy the human needs in "paradise."

As an example, there was the man who took care of the dolphins (yes, dolphins!)

and lived at the hotel. We became acquainted and exchanged brief life histories as I watched him put his pets through their morning routines. He had renounced his church and his childhood faith, and he was quite bitter on the subject. "I've turned my back on all that," he announced to my husband and me—and sought us out frequently to reiterate the point. It became part of our daily conversations for Jack to challenge us: "What about this Bible discrepancy?" and quote a passage out of context.

Finally, one day I said, "Jack, I think Jesus is simply waiting for you to come back. And I think you would like to go back to your church. If you were truly 'through with all that,' as you claim to be, it wouldn't be bothering you so much."

Jack evidently thought that over carefully, for before we left he had made an appointment to visit the minister of his church. We had really only acted as the catalyst that gave him the courage to act. Our interest provided the small nudge that started the lost sheep back on his way.

There was also Mrs. Grove, world traveler. She was a skeptic—cynical but deeply in need of something firm in which to believe. She wasn't yet ready to accept Christ as the answer. But when she asked for my itinerary so she could continue our talks, it was clear that she had discovered something of value in "my" Christianity and was going to pursue the matter further. "I just need more time to understand it all," she concluded.

The hotel had its share of famous guests. They were in Kobola to "hide out," as they expressed it. I was intimidated by their fame, I admit. I felt restraint around them. I rationalized by telling myself that I had no business prying into their private lives. On reflection, too late, I find that rather silly. Many drank too heavily and looked anything but relaxed and happy in the beautiful surroundings. I have no doubt those people are searching, too. Another time I would pray for a boldness to approach them as God's people, rather than be awed by them as "special" in human terms.

But God did perhaps direct me toward one couple who in spite of their wealth and position were silently seeking help. Mr. and Mrs. Vine were in their late forties, charming, friendly, and gracious.

Mr. Vine was quite relaxed and prepared to enjoy himself, but Mrs. Vine was obviously a chronic worrier. Her mind was still at home in California. Their "vacation" was not serving its purpose in her case at all.

It seems that after their own children had grown, Mrs. Vine had felt lost in her "empty nest." In a series of attempts to fill the void in her life, she had adopted not one but five children over the last few years. The Vines were now middle-aged parents of a lively young family, and the strain was written clearly on Mrs. Vine's face.

"I'm glad you are taking some time out to play," I laughingly commented one day.

"It's the first time in two years I've gotten Betty away from home," Bill Vine answered.

"But our youngest is only four, and he has problems, and I worry about him," she insisted.

Bill Vine sounded a little impatient as he said, "We have a governess and a housekeeper. They are taking perfectly good care of everything. Still my wife worries."

"You are going to have to let God take over your worries," I suggested.

"Oh, I do," she quickly replied. "We all regularly attend church."

Once again I repeated what had become almost a cliche: "Attending church is always commendable, but the ultimate is Christianity, not churchianity."

"I never thought of it that way before," Betty said thoughtfully.

"God will take over our worries if we let Him, and in exchange He will give us peace," I continued. During our few days' acquaintance we talked more—about values and priorities as well as God's peace versus man's anxieties.

I wish I could tell you that at the end of our stay Betty was a carefree, happy woman. But I can't. She still struggled with her need for human effort—and the continual human incapacity to "do it alone."

This, however, is an ongoing story. Next spring I am to visit the Vines in their home. Who knows?—by then Betty and God may have formed a working relationship that will benefit the whole family. In the meantime, I shall listen—by phone and mail—and encourage.

In retrospect it seems that God did indeed plan for us to share our faith while enjoying a bit of earthly "paradise."

Points to Consider

1. One can see many differences between a small-town church supper and a gathering around a pool at the Kobola Hilton. What similarities strike you?
2. Are we ever justified in taking a "vacation" just for our own entertainment? Discuss.

Chapter **17**

Mr. Juarez — Above Tragedy

"Listen to this," said my friend Mary, holding up a newspaper. "Mr. Juarez struggles to keep family together—wife dies in childbirth leaving infant and five other children—Mr. Juarez refuses to give up family for adoption—'I will use up all my savings to stay home and take care of them,' he says."

"My heart really goes out to someone like that," said Mary. "I'm going to see if I can organize some projects and give that family a helping hand." Competent soul that she was, Mary followed through and did what she could to help the Juarez family.

One of her voluntary efforts was to drive the children to Sunday school. When he thought the baby was old enough to go to the nursery, Mr. Juarez came to the services also. I can still picture him seated in the back row with his five dark-eyed children. He had not been in our country very long when tragedy had entered his life.

Sunday after Sunday he listened intently to words of encouragement from the Bible. It took all his concentration just to understand the language. He certainly understood the message, though. One memorable Sunday morning he bravely left that back row, marched to the front of the sanctuary, and exclaimed, "I need your Jesus in my life!"

Our congregation (which, frankly, was a trifle on the stuffy side) gasped. But Carlos Juarez had seen Christ at work in other lives, and when Carlos believed in something, he acted.

He took his newfound Christianity just as seriously as he took his family responsibilities. His sister came from Mexico to take over the care of the children, and Carlos was able to go back to his job as a chef. The Juarez household was running smoothly now, and we all were glad for them. As Carlos commented, "I can handle anything, now that Jesus is my partner!"

But just when everything was going so well, tragedy struck again. Carlos became ill and discovered he had cancer—he would only live a few more months. It seemed unfair that this young man (only 34), who was so vital to so many children, should be taken away.

But Carlos Juarez did not waste time feeling sorry for himself. He quite sensibly realized that he had no time to waste. With Jesus beside him (and Carlos had a very personal picture of "his Jesus" beside him), he set his affairs in order. He arranged that upon his death all six children would go—together—to a Christian children's home. In return, the oldest daughter, now a high-school senior, would act as a helper to the staff. His family would remain a family, even though he and his wife hadn't been granted long lives to watch their children grow up.

Once Carlos had provided for his children as best he could, he quite literally turned his eyes toward Heaven. He was excited to be going—to see his wife and his parents again—and actually to meet "his Jesus." Soon he was hospitalized, and he certainly didn't lack visitors. Many of the people who had been shocked on the day of his "conversion" now loved him dearly. They hastened to comfort him in his last days. But each time someone visited Carlos, the visitor would be the one to go away comforted by the joyful man awaiting his big adventure. It was as though he had completed his earthly responsibilities and was again an eager child on his way to his true home.

Yes, our church reached out to help Carlos Juarez when he needed it—and in return he taught all of us a deeper kind of faith.

Points to Consider

1. As written here, this is basically a happy story. Do you agree?
2. How do you react when someone expresses his faith in an unconventional way? Are you suspicious? Shocked? Interested?
3. Do you think Carlos was realistic or idealistic?

Chapter **18**

Louise — A Job Done Well

Louise was a classic example of single-minded determination. I met her when I was taking a survey in her rather shabby neighborhood. Hers was the conspicuously neat, scrubbed house on the don't-care street. As I approached it, I half expected to be greeted by a dour little widow who was grimly "making ends meet." Instead, I narrowly escaped a hurtling football—Louise was a good punter! She and her son were having a little practice, but she welcomed me and invited me in for a chat. She seemed genuinely pleased that I had interrupted her activities and was now drinking her tea and munching her cookies. Her two children were polite, eager, and helpful. This was obviously a happy and close family.

In our conversation I learned that Louise's husband was seldom home. "He has a drinking problem," she said in a matter-of-fact way, "but we are working on it." Louise was not looking for sympathy. She had one primary goal, and that was to give her children the best life possible under the circumstances. "I have to be mother and father to them most of the time," was the way she put it.

Louise and I became friends after our first meeting. One day while we were talking, I asked her what she thought about Jesus Christ. She obviously hadn't thought much about Him at all, but her answer was characteristic of everything she did—"If Christ can help me be a better mother to my children, I would be foolish to refuse to accept His help. It's certain I need all the help I can get to direct this family."

Christ not only became her Savior, but He became her confidante and comfort as she progressed through her busy days. She worked at whatever she could to bring in a little extra money—as long as she could be home when the children were.

Not only was Louise a conscientious mother, she was a wise and good one. Though her children were overwhelmingly important to her, she did not hover over them or cater to any childish whims and complaints. Neither did she tolerate any criticism of their father. Somehow, though her resources were hardly above the poverty level, she managed to keep a spirit of joy in what could have been a very depressing situation.

Once Christ joined the family, Louise extended herself even further. She became a Sunday-school teacher, and her way with children benefited many of us. She often acted as my baby-sitter, though I had to be home at the end of school hours so she could go and greet her own children. This was their time for sharing, talking, and even football—and nothing took precedence over that.

I knew Louise for several years. During

that time her husband continued to be more of a liability than an asset, but she continued to work around the situation, refrained from nagging or judging him, and maintained a cheerful Christian home for the children.

Neither child was particularly brilliant, but both finished school in creditable fashion. Her daughter married and today is the heart of her own Christian family—fortunately in this case the husband is also a strong Christian and a good provider. Louise's son is also married, and he and his family have gone to the mission field. He works as a carpenter, sharing the Christian message with those who work beside him.

As the children grew up, Louise shared her gift for "mothering" with her church, even becoming Sunday-school superintendent. We all rejoiced to see this diligent mother ultimately reaping the fruit of her labors.

Points to Consider

1. What do you think of Louise's motive for becoming a Christian?
2. Do you see any evidence that would indicate the role religion played in her life?
3. Do you feel sorry for Louise? Why or why not?

Chapter 19

The Bradleys — The "Surprise" Party

I met Elaine Bradley at a neighborhood coffee, but our initial encounter was not particularly warm. It was hard to get acquainted with her. She seemed aloof and preoccupied with her own affairs. "Totally disinterested in what the rest of us are doing" was the assessment I passed along to my husband when I got home.

I ran into her from time to time, and I made a special effort to be friendly. Her son was in my kindergarten class, so it was always easy to find a topic of conversation! Bit by bit she responded. She still didn't seek me out, but she was at least willing to chat occasionally. She even came to a few of our church's social functions.

Elaine's husband Jim and my husband became friends also. They were both licensed pilots. Besides this my husband, a farmer at heart, loved to visit Jim who was currently running a farm he had inherited.

As long as our conversations revolved about farming and flying, kids and kindergarten, we enjoyed a pleasant friendship. The Bradleys had made it very clear, however, that they were not interested in any "spiritual probing." They attended an occasional church service or Sunday-school program that involved their children, but that was it.

For about a year the relationship went along in this vein. Then one day I dropped in to see Elaine and found her flurrying around excitedly. "For one night, at least, I'm going to shake this farm dust off my feet!" she announced, waving an engraved invitation in front of me.

"My sorority is having a reunion—and it's a full-fledged formal bash at the Crystal Inn. My dress has to be let out—wouldn't you know—but I can hardly wait for Friday night. We haven't gone to a really big party since we moved out here into the cornfields." She laughed. "There won't be any pious types at this gathering!"

That I could believe. The Crystal Inn was not noted for piety, or, quite frankly, respectability. Elaine definitely expected me to be shocked, or at least mildly disapproving.

"Perhaps I can help you with the dress," was my comment.

"Oh—thank you," was her somewhat surprised reply.

We worked on her dress most of the afternoon. As we worked she enumerated all the people who would be there—friends she hadn't seen since college, and certainly not since she had become a farmer's wife.

When Friday came, the Bradleys stopped by for a moment on their way to the dance. They were a handsome couple, and at the moment they were looking their best. "Stop by for coffee tomorrow morning and I'll give you a complete rundown," Elaine promised.

Saturday morning, on the late side, I rang Elaine's doorbell. I was met by a very sober, subdued hostess. We settled down with our coffee cups, and I prepared to listen—for Elaine obviously had something to tell.

This time *she* surprised *me*. "I've finally got things put together," was her opening remark. "You may not have realized it, but in the past I've been totally turned off by Christians. Both Jim and I have had bad experiences with so-called 'Christians' who insisted on cramming their beliefs down our throats the minute we showed the slightest interest.

"You and your husband have been different. You have liked us for what we are, and you haven't pestered us about religion. You've just been good friends.

"Well, maybe more of your kind of life has rubbed off on us than we realized. At least, we sure found out that last night wasn't what we had anticipated at all."

I continued to listen as Elaine talked. Apparently most of the crowd wasn't sober enough to be even decently sociable. The Crystal Inn had lived up to its tacky reputation, and Jim and Elaine had come home early.

"I can't believe it, but we had a better time at your church Halloween party than at that dance last night!" Elaine concluded. "We just don't fit in with that life any more."

There was little I could add to what Elaine had said. God had used our way of life rather than our sermons to reach out to Jim and Elaine. But reach He had, and accept they did. Their "big evening" had surpassed their wildest expectations in terms of happiness received—the lasting kind.

Points to Consider
1. Why do you think Elaine was aloof when we first met? There may have been several reasons.
2. If someone seems unfriendly to you, do you tend to take it personally or are you likely to be extra friendly in return? What motivates your reaction?

Chapter **20**

Stephanie — One Link in the Chain

I still remember one particular Sunday morning, though it was many years ago. I was rushing around the house, madly searching for my son's left shoe. My daughter was complaining about going out so early in the cold rain, as only five-year-olds can complain. "Well, shoe or no shoe, we've got to get going," I can remember saying. "Get in the car."

And why was I, who lived next door to the church, dragging my half-dressed children around town an hour before Sunday school was even scheduled to begin? As we bumped along a little dirt road, muddy and slippery that day, I asked the same question. What was I accomplishing by all this?

My errand was one I had been doing every Sunday morning, rain or shine, for over a year. At this point in my life I was teaching in a public junior high. One of my students, a girl from a cultured but unchurched family, had expressed an interest in coming to our Sunday school, if only she had a way to get there. Of course I had offered to provide the way. Here was a child who wanted to know God. The least I could do was give her a ride to church.

Each Sunday I would pick up Stephanie, bright and eager, her Sunday-school lesson beautifully prepared. As I did so, her parents would get into their car and drive off to their place of business. They appreciated my interest in their daughter, but they were totally disinterested in anything to do with religion.

On this morning I actually resented my obligation. My own children were inconvenienced, and I certainly was inconvenienced. Why couldn't Stephanie's parents drop her off on their way to work? Why couldn't they see how important God was becoming in her life?

Even as these thoughts swirled through my head, I knew the answers to my questions. For whatever reasons, Stephanie's parents were not going to take her to church. God seemed to feel that this was my job. And of course I *had* volunteered. Very well, I would not become "weary in well doing."

Every Sunday for another year I continued to drive the extra five miles down the bumpy road to pick up Stephanie. Most of the time the ride didn't seem to be a chore at all, though inevitably there were a few reruns of that bleak Sunday morning. Stephanie was eager to learn about Jesus and to accept Him as her Savior. That in itself was enough reward.

Finally our family moved, and our connection with Stephanie and her family ended. I often thought of my little passenger and hoped that somehow she had persevered in the faith she had found, but I had no idea what had become of her until last summer, almost twenty years later.

I was attending a church service in the area where we had formerly lived. I didn't know many of the people there, after such a long absence, but something about the lady singer seemed familiar. As she sang, I tried to figure out who she might be. Suddenly I knew—this was Stephanie's mother, the lady who never went to church!

After the service, a friend pieced together the story for me. It seems that Stephanie had continued to go to church and Sunday school all through her high-school years, enrolled in a Christian college, and eventually married a medical missionary. Gradually her Christian influence had begun to change her family. Her parents at last became interested, found the Christian faith for themselves, and now were active church members. Next the grandparents accepted Christ, and through them a brother and sister-in-law of Stephanie's mother. Six additional people were now active Christians, all because of the influence of one little girl. And since that girl was now working on the mission field, who could begin to estimate her ultimate impact?

I couldn't help but think as I listened to

the story of how tempted I had been to abandon my part in it. In strictly human terms, it might have made more sense if I just stayed home on Sunday mornings and helped my own children look for lost shoes. I thank God for letting me see the situation in His terms instead.

Points to Consider

1. Have you ever nobly begun a project and found it becoming a burden as time went by? Did you abandon it or "keep plugging"? What influenced your decision?
2. How would you balance my inconvenience against the end result?
3. We have no guarantee that any given effort will produce a given result. Given that fact, and the fact of your faith in God, how do you determine your own priorities? (Good question for group discussion.)

Chapter 21

Heather — Lost, One Coat; Found, One Friend

Breathlessly I rushed onto the plane, literally fell into my seat, and sank back to relax. Getting from my hotel to the airport had been a frantic process involving cabs, a bus, and the Los Angeles traffic. But I had made it with five minutes to spare. Now I could just sit and listen to soothing music.

The soothing music was almost immediately interrupted by a weather announcement: "The temperature in Chicago is 32° and cloudy."

"Oh, no!" I said aloud. I had just realized that the garment bag containing my coat was still hanging in the hotel closet. I shivered at the thought.

It was then that I noticed a similarly distressed-looking passenger at the other end of our four-seat row. She was wearing only jeans and a light shirt, and she looked as unhappy as I was feeling. "It's going to be cold when we get off this plane," I ventured, "and I don't even have a coat with me."

"Neither do I," the girl answered. "This is all I have with me, and I'm going all the way to Boston." She looked frightened, fragile, and lonely.

"Did you forget your luggage, too?" I asked.

"No." She hesitated a moment, then continued, "I'm sort of running away." As she spoke I could see that she was fighting back tears.

"Want to talk about it?" I asked. Immediately she moved over to the empty seat next to me. She obviously was in distress and desperately hoping to find a sympathetic ear. "My name is Heather," she said as we introduced ourselves.

"Maybe I can help her," I thought. "I'm older and wiser—perhaps she is looking for spiritual insights. How should I begin?" As I silently said a brief prayer for wisdom, God seemed to answer, "Don't talk, just listen."

And listen I did. I listened and listened.

Here was a girl who seemed to have everything money could buy. "My father gives me everything he can think of," she said, "but the cost is too great. He wants to control my life. He even wants to do my thinking for me. I'm going to college and I got a part-time job in a bank. He's trying to make me quit the job. He says he wants me to be a student—but I'm already getting straight A's. Really, he just doesn't want me to earn my own money. He wants to own me just like he owns everything else.

"I'm twenty-two years old, and I can't take any more of his ways. I would be able to get along without any of his money—I can work my way through school—it will just take longer. Everything he gives me has strings attached—and I've had it!"

Her tale went on. She had spent the night with a girl friend, called a sympathetic aunt in Boston, and was now flying there to get away for awhile and think things out. The trip was costing her almost a thousand dollars, everything she had saved from her salary at the bank. "I don't think I can live at home anymore," she said. "I want to go to school, and keep my job, and do my own thinking. I'm through being a puppet!"

"Can't you make your father understand how you feel about him?" I asked. "You are an adult, you know."

"Not to him," she answered. "He called all my friends last night trying to find out where I had gone. He even called the bank to see if they knew where I was. One other time when I tried to stand up to him, and told him I wanted to live without his money or his domination, he hounded me until I just gave up. This time, I'm determined not to let him even know where I am."

It was obvious that communication between Heather and her father was at an impasse. Judging from her manner and what she told me, she seemed to be a diligent student, conservative in her behavior, and willing to be a good, obedient daughter—to a point. Her father, it appeared, had the classic attitude that he who controls the purse controls everything. More than likely he was still unprepared to see his little girl grow up. He had not learned that to hold a child one must first let the child go.

Eventually Heather talked herself out. In the process she had revealed that the family was of a non-Christian religion, though I had no idea how sincerely they practiced their faith.

"I could give you many answers, but there is really only One who can help you," I said. "I respect your faith, and I know you may not agree with me." She made no comment, so I continued. "I can only share with you the inner peace I have found in my own life. Jesus Christ has given me that peace, and He helps me to cope with all the problems that come up."

Heather said, "Well, I really have no deep convictions about my religion. It's my father who talks religion at our house, but there's too big a gap between his creed and deed to convince me of anything." Again her hostility was evident; her voice was bitter.

"Jesus Christ can fill our hearts with love so that we can love even our enemies," I persisted. "And the beautiful thing is that we have such peace through it all. People we couldn't even like for themselves become lovable when we see them in His terms."

"You make Jesus sound very personal," Heather said.

"You're very discerning," I observed. "It was only when I asked Christ to take over my mixed-up will and emotions that He became personal. And when I started reading the Bible I found out more what He was like and what He wanted me to do."

"It seems to make a lot of sense," Heather said, rather wistfully.

I decided I had talked enough for now. "Why don't you try to get some sleep?" I suggested. I was sure she had had very little rest during the past twenty-four hours. "And one other thing! Don't you think you'll feel better if you let your father know you're safe and only going to be gone a few days? He must be terribly worried; because in his own way I'm sure he must love you a great deal."

"I think I will, once I get to my aunt's

house," said Heather drowsily. Within minutes she was sleeping beside me, exhausted.

As I looked at the pensive little face, I could only pray that what I had said would help her begin to find her way. Was there anything else I could do?

Yes—and perhaps this was providential. My brother-in-law is a Christian counselor at her college. I could contact him. Perhaps he could manage to meet her and help her after she returned to the campus. How? If past history is any indication, God will provide the way.

Points to Consider
1. What do you see as the biggest problem—Heather, her father, or their interrelationship?
2. Would you feel uncomfortable talking about Jesus to someone whose background is non-Christian? How would you approach such a discussion?